Managing Well

Managers are crucial to the success of organizations. While companies invest heavily on educat...

Prepare for Development

- business management
- people management
- process management
- communication
- personal effectiveness.

Note that this issue is not intended to be a replace-
ment for traditional management development; it
is a guide to help you identify areas for improvement and plan for development as well as a sup-
plement to any formal learning programs offered
by your organization.

Competencies

Once you have identified where you could use
some improvement and determined which competencies have caused the most pain in the past, your
next step is to improve your skills. The following
sections provide brief overviews of the competencies as well as some tools, practices, and habits that
can be useful in your quest to become a better
manager. Feel free to skip some competencies and
focus on others.

Management Competencies Self-Assessment

Consider the following statements and rate yourself on them according to the following key: (5) This is a real strength; (3) I have adequate skills in this area; (1) I could use some improvement in this area. Then add up your scores for each competency. Circle the three or four competencies with the lowest scores to focus on and assign priority to them (A, B, C).

Business Management	5	3	1	Priority (A, B, C)
I can describe my organization's goals and competitive environment.				
I understand principles of finance, budgeting, and accounting.				
I am skilled at preparing strategic plans that align with organizational goals.				
I understand relevant business regulations and procedures in my organization's industry.				
BUSINESS MANAGEMENT TOTAL:				
People Management				
I use an effective process to hire employees.				
I work with my employees to identify performance goals for them that align with the organization's goals.				
I am comfortable delegating work to my employees.				
I enable my employees to achieve their performance goals and more through effective coaching and motivation techniques.				
PEOPLE MANAGEMENT TOTAL:				
Process Management				
I run effective meetings that achieve their stated goals.				
I understand how change affects people and how to help them to embrace it.				
I am skilled at planning, organizing, and controlling work.				
I use resources effectively.				
PROCESS MANAGEMENT TOTAL:				

Communication	5	3	1	Priority (A, B, C)
I communicate well orally.				
I withhold judgment until I have completely and accurately heard what someone intends to say.				
I regularly provide both constructive and positive feedback that is specific and immediate.				
I communicate well in writing.				
COMMUNICATION TOTAL:				
Personal Effectiveness				
I practice excellent time management skills.				
Each day, I choose to first work on tasks that are highest priority to the organization and to me.				
My work space is well organized, and I always know where to find documents I need.				
I use effective problem-solving and decision-making processes.				
PERSONAL EFFECTIVENESS TOTAL:				

Business Management

According to Lisa Haneberg in "Reinventing Middle Management," today's managers "see themselves as business owners" and "know that they create and represent the organization; they establish the work context." In light of this, the need for a broad understanding of the organization as well as specific knowledge of business regulations and procedures becomes clear. The following are some examples of business knowledge you should know.

■ *State of the Business*
As a manager, you need to understand your organization's

● *business model,* which describes how an organization plans to serve its customers and its employees and includes both strategy and implementation plans

● *business objectives,* which state what your organization wants to accomplish; for example, a business objective might be to increase profitability by five percent in the next year with the launch of a new product

● *factors that affect organizational growth,* including the competitive environment and the industry as well as the current culture and values of an organization

● *business drivers,* which are the internal (for example, product development) and external forces (for example, government or technology) that direct an organization's strategy, goals, business needs, and performance needs.

To complete the picture of the state of the business, you also need to understand corporate success measures and how the organization defines and measures success. All these factors determine how you will link your department's goals and objectives to overall business goals and objectives.

Basic Accounting Terms

To work effectively with your accounting department or with executives in the organization, you need to understand and learn to use basic accounting terminology.

- **Assets** refer to economic resources—in other words, what a company owns—that may be expressed in monetary terms.

- **Liabilities** are the debts or expenses a company owes.

- **Equity** is the value of the owners' or shareholders' portion of the business after all claims against it.

- **Balance sheet** is a statement of the firm's financial position, including assets, liabilities, and equity (liabilities + equity = assets).

- **Income statements** explain revenues, expenses, and profits over a specified period of time (revenues - expenses = net income).

- **Chart of accounts** is the listing of account lines maintained in the general ledger.

- **Cost-benefit analysis** is a comparison that weighs the costs of a training activity against the outcomes achieved and is carried out to determine the return-on-investment.

- **Expenses** are the costs incurred in the process of earning revenues and conducting business.

- **Incurred expenses** are the expenses in which obligations have been fulfilled but not paid.

- **Operating expenses** are expenses that relate directly to business operations, not to providing products or services.

- **Revenue** is the money a company earns by providing goods or services to its customers.

- **Financial statements** are the four statements that show the end results of an organization's financial condition: balance sheet, income statement, statement of cash flows, and statement of owners' equity.

Some ways you can identify these components of your organization include

- reviewing the organization's mission and vision statements and its annual report

- reviewing strategic plans (these will often be confidential) and talking to executives about the strategic direction of the organization

- maintaining knowledge of your industry through trade papers, conferences, and so forth.

■ **Budgeting and Accounting**

Creating a good budget is more than an annual event designed to document spending; it's a working plan that guides fiscal decisions. A well-designed and executed budget forms the foundation for developing next year's budget.

Although budgeting is often referred to as a process, in reality it's part of a larger accounting system (for some basic accounting terms, see the sidebar at left). A typical accounting system includes three steps:

1. Budget design and development (forecasting).

2. Budget execution (expense tracking, monitoring, and management).

3. Reporting and reconciliation.

In an optimal planning process, you would design a budget based on the business plan, not on other factors, such as available revenue to fund the plan or previous spending levels. The assumption is that business goals justify the expenditures. Note that it is good practice to work with your organization's accounting department to learn their preferences in terms of processes and documentation; this may help you to avoid having to redo your work.

■ **Organizational Structure**

Organizational structure refers to both formal and informal reporting structures as well as ways that information moves across the organization and work gets done. You can learn about formal structures from organization charts, but understanding informal structures requires personal observation and keeping your ear open. However, knowing the informal ways that things get done in an organization can be very powerful. For example, knowing who influences whom can be useful knowledge if you need to get something done.

■ *Strategic Planning*

Strategic planning can be defined as the process of systematically organizing the future, a process in which managers and other professionals use past experience as a filter for future decisions. When creating a strategic plan for your department, focus attention on department outcomes that link with the overall organization's mission and strategic plan and address these questions:

- Where is my department now?

- Where does my department want to go?

- How will my department get there?

- What are my department's strengths and weaknesses?

You can develop a strategic plan by using a four-phase process (see the sidebar *Strategic Planning* at right). Use strategic planning as a tool to accomplish more things that are critical to your department and to the overall business strategy. For that reason, don't think of strategic planning as a one-time event; it should be an ongoing process.

■ *Business Regulations*

Another important component of the business management competency is knowledge of business regulations and ethics. These may include

- employment law and regulatory requirements
- civil rights legislation
- workplace safety
- securities and financial reporting
- information technology compliance
- union relations
- intellectual property
- corporate policies and procedures
- ethical standards.

You can find information about these regulations through your human resources department, government websites, and any professional associations that you may belong to.

Strategic Planning

As a manager, you must be able to turn organizational goals into department goals. The way to do this is to carry out strategic planning for your department. Use this four-phase model to help you.

Phase	Task
1. Formulation	• Identify organizational mission, vision, and values. • Develop department mission, vision, and value statements based on this organizational review.
2. Development	• Conduct an analysis of strengths, weaknesses, opportunities, and threats (SWOT). • Establish strategic goals (two to three years to attain). • Identify strategies to attain those goals.
3. Implementation	• Establish long-term measurable goals to achieve strategies. • Establish short-term objectives (six months to a year) for each goal. • Create action plans to achieve those objectives. • Allocate resources to work toward those objectives. • Motivate employees to achieve those objectives.
4. Evaluation	• Review strategies. • Measure actual performance against strategies, goals, and objectives. • Take corrective action.

For more information on strategic planning, see "Managing the Strategic Planning Process," *Infoline* No. 259710, and "Strategic Planning for Human Resource Development," *Infoline* No. 259206.

Hiring Checklist

Hiring top performers is the culmination of effective recruitment and advertising, interviewing, and selecting. The following four areas cover the basics of the process.

Area 1: Requirements

☐ Focus on the few key attributes you are looking for.

☐ Have a plan. You must see how your employee needs link to the strategic plan of the organization.

☐ Look for *organizational* fit—not just job fit.

☐ Specify the job. Be clear about what the job entails.

Area 2: Hiring System

☐ Plan and prepare for interviews. Eliminate unnecessary duplication of questions, practice your approach, and test your questions beforehand.

☐ Develop the same basic questions for each interview so there will be a basis for comparison later on.

☐ Use both open-ended and closed-ended questions in an interview. Plan on talking about 25 percent of the time and listening about 75 percent of the time.

Area 3: Basics

☐ Be a good host. For example, make the interviewee feel welcome and offer refreshment.

☐ Make sure the interview and hiring processes are clear up front.

☐ Hone your interviewing skills and review federal guidelines for interviewing.

Area 4: Value-Added System

☐ Relate the interview to values and vision, not just to job experience.

☐ Meet across functions with people who will work with this person.

☐ Have a way to compare meaningful notes afterward.

Adapted from E. Stewart Hickman's "Hiring and Retaining Top Performing Employees," Infoline No. 250011.

People Management

The ability to manage people well is a crucial competency for managers, especially given that the job of managers is to achieve the goals of the department and the organization through the work of other people. Furthermore, it has become a truism that people don't leave organizations; people leave managers. How people are managed is a crucial factor in retaining employees.

For these reasons, it's important to develop strong people management skills. Some of these are discussed in the following sections.

Hiring and Retaining

How well your people perform starts with how well you selected them in the first place, and there are effective processes you can learn to interview candidates and hire the right employees (see the sidebar *Hiring Checklist* at left for an overview of an effective hiring process).

To prepare to interview candidates, ask yourself three questions:

1. What will make a candidate suitable for this job?

2. What are the signals that a candidate may be suitable for the job?

3. What are the signals that a candidate may not be suitable for the job?

Preparing an answer to the first question in advance will enable you to answer the second two during the interview itself. Although you will use the job description as a resource, note that the first question refers to more than job requirements; it refers to the culture of your organization and your department. In other words, what kind of person represents a good fit?

Once you have hired the right person, you need to work to retain that person. Losing employees is costly and disruptive to the smooth functioning of your department. One way to do this is to model your department on organizations with good track records for retention, which share certain characteristics. They

- value their workers

- tie workforce initiatives to organizational strategies

- understand the importance of employee growth and development

- link training to operations

- provide training and development for everyone

- use competencies

- track, measure, and evaluate their initiatives.

Managing Performance

Managing employees' performance goes beyond completing a performance review once or twice a year. Although formal performance reviews are an important tool in developing individual goals that will enable the department and ultimately the organization to achieve their goals, managing employees' performance should take place on a far more frequent basis, ideally weekly, or even daily.

This high level of engagement has become increasingly rare, according to Bruce Tulgan in "The Under-Management Epidemic," and represents a fear on the part of managers to appear to be the dreaded micromanager. Tulgan notes "that these under-managers often think they are being 'good guys' by soft-pedaling their authority, but their failure to provide leadership causes so many problems that they are not being good guys at all."

Tulgan describes these six characteristics of highly successful and engaged managers:

1. They know a lot about their employees' work, including how much, how fast, and how hard.

2. They have regular meetings with every employee, ideally once a day, but at a minimum, once a week, to talk about how the job is going.

3. They write everything down in a manager's notebook, which is a running log of employee meetings.

4. They do a lot for their employees—for example, provide training opportunities, recognition, different schedule arrangements—but they expect a lot in return.

5. They link rewards to specific instances of high performance.

6. They consider high performance to be the only option and work hard to achieve it through clear performance expectations, regular feedback, coaching for development, frank discussions, planning, and termination, if required.

Delegating

Delegation is often billed as a time-saving mechanism for the manager, but its benefits don't stop there. Successful delegation maximizes an organization's output, while producing competent employees, balanced budgets, and promotable managers. "Managers who delegate properly will always accomplish more than those who refuse to let go of projects their subordinates should be doing," says Eugene Raudsepp in "How to Delegate Effectively." Delegation has two goals: First, to free you up from routine tasks so that you can focus on more big-picture strategic tasks and, second, to develop employee skills so that they are learning and preparing for future tasks and positions.

Here is an effective process for delegating tasks:

- Decide what to delegate by identifying tasks that someone else can do just as well. (However, remember to always retain tasks related to overall planning, policy making, goal setting, budget supervision, confidential information, and subordinate relations.)

- Pick the right person for the task. To do this, consider your subordinates' characteristics, skills, and interests. The perfect assignment will challenge, but not overwhelm, your employee.

- Plan carefully and explain clearly. Communicate your priorities (speed or quality, for example), expected results, and performance criteria.

- Delegate both responsibility and authority. Make sure the employee has what he or she needs to get the job done. In the area of authority, that may mean contacting others with whom the employee will be working, requesting their cooperation, and letting them know the employee has full authority to complete the task.

- Monitor progress regularly, especially with employees who are undertaking unfamiliar assignments.

- Delegate a whole project. The employee will gain far more satisfaction and learn more from carrying out a complete project than he or she will from doing bits and pieces. If that isn't possible, explain the relevance of his or her contribution to the overall project.

- Encourage your employee. Provide constructive feedback and coaching as required.

- Evaluate the project together with the employee. Correct mistakes privately and tactfully, and reward success generously.

Motivating

Motivation is defined as a psychological force that determines what a person chooses to do, how hard he or she works, and how persistent he or she is in the face of a challenge. Understanding a variety of motivational theories and the different ways that different people are motivated is crucial to the successful work of a manager. The following two influences have a great effect on the motivation of your employees and should also be considered when integrating motivation into work planning, performance feedback, and relationship building:

- ***Management Recognition***
Instead of coming from some nebulous, ad hoc committee or corporate institution, the most valuable recognition comes directly from a person's manager. The sidebar *Rewarding Employees* provides a sampling of ways that you can reward your employees.

- ***Performance Incentives***
Your employees want to be recognized for the jobs they were hired to do. The most effective incentives are based on job performance—not on non-performance-related praise such as attendance.

Developing People

According to Haneberg, today's effective managers create work environments in which employees thrive. One important way to accomplish this is to provide challenging opportunities to learn and grow as well as to provide coaching and feedback.

To be a successful coach, you need to demonstrate certain behaviors, such as supporting employees' needs, creating choices, seeking commitment, and providing avenues of self-expression. Work toward a balance between being supportive and caring and being clear and direct about what is expected of the employee. Two categories of coaching behaviors are effective in developing employees: supporting behaviors and initiating behaviors.

Supporting behaviors demonstrate caring, concern, and acceptance and lead to reduced tension and more open communication. Examples include

- collaboration on solutions to problem areas
- help and assistance where needed
- concern about worker's needs and objectives
- empathy.

Initiating behaviors encourage the employee to discuss the work situation. A manager's initiating behaviors include

- providing feedback and analysis of issues
- clarifying goals and expectations
- planning solutions and changes
- outlining consequences of employee actions.

Process Management

Three processes are familiar to most managers: meeting management, change management, and project management. The following sections will describe some effective methods and tools to carry these out.

Meeting Management

Ineffective meetings that don't achieve their goals are some of the biggest time and money wasters in organizations today. Furthermore, they waste employee commitment and energy.

To make the most of meeting time, you need to do some planning and preparation. Before the meeting, you should

- determine what the meeting should accomplish

- identify who needs to be there and what he or she needs to do to prepare for the meeting

- prepare an agenda

- identify any tools you may need (whiteboards, markers, and so forth)

- invite participants, providing them with a description of what the meeting should achieve as well as any pre-work to accomplish.

At the time of the meeting, you should

- ensure that you have the space and tools that you need

- start on time

- introduce the participants to each other

- explain why you are meeting

Rewarding Employees

Research into why talented people stay in organizations is the basis for the following ways to show your employees that you appreciate them:

■ ***Private Time With You***
Have lunch with an employee and ask questions like, "What can I do to keep you on my team?" "What might make your work life easier?" "What can I do to be more supportive to help you?"

■ ***Frank Talk About the Future***
Hold a career conversation in a quiet, private place—off-site, if possible. Ask the following questions to start: "What do you enjoy most about your job? The least?" "Which of your talents have I not used yet?" "What jobs do you see yourself doing in the future?"

■ ***Potential Growth***
Let employees choose from a list of potential projects, assignments, or tasks that could enrich their work.

■ ***Submit to Pruning***
Ask the employee with whom you never agree to engage in some straight talk about how you can work together better. Listen carefully and don't defend yourself. Then take a step toward changing at least one behavior.

■ ***A Unique Perk for Fun***
Give an employee a "kicks" coupon that entitles him or her to spend up to X amount of money to take a break or have some fun at work. It could involve the whole team.

■ ***Blending Work and Passion***
Have a "Passion Breakfast" for all employees, a team, or one on one. Ask, "What do you love to do?" "At work?" "Outside of work?" Brainstorm and commit to helping them build more of what they love into their workday.

■ ***Genie in a Bottle***
Ask an employee to write down six ways he or she would like to be rewarded. Anything goes. The only rule is that half of the ideas have to be low or no cost.

■ ***A Chance to Download***
Give 12 coupons for listening time—one for each month, in which an employee can talk about anything for 20 minutes. Your job isn't to understand, just to listen.

Adapted from Beverly L. Kaye and Sharon Jordan-Evans's "The ABCs of Management Gift-Giving," Training &Development, December 2000.

- forecast the meeting process

- explain the ground rules

- display enthusiasm.

During the meeting, use meeting facilitation skills to keep to the agenda, ask all participants to contribute, and park topics that are not on the agenda.

And always follow up meetings by typing up notes and distributing them to everyone who participated, planning to follow up on commitments made in the meeting, and plan for a follow-up meeting to ensure that commitments are being upheld.

Change Management

Organizations make the decision to change for business reasons. But how change is implemented is based on "people reasons." It is important for managers to understand reactions to change and how to implement change effectively.

An organization's people are a critical component in ensuring that any organizational change initiative is successful. Management consultant, futurist, speaker, and prolific author Karl Albrecht described the *personal change response cycle* to help individuals work though the progressive psychological phases of change response, which are as follows:

■ *Threat*
In this phase, individuals are afraid to change the status quo because of fear of the unknown or fear of a state worse than the status quo.

■ *Problem*
At this point, individuals perceive change to be a lot of work and problems. Because they no longer know the rules, it's difficult for them to complete their jobs.

■ *Solution*
Overcoming the problems perceived in the previous phase starts to reveal some of the benefits of the change.

■ *Habit*
As old operating procedures are forgotten, the new become the norm.

Individuals progress through these phases at different rates. Your job as manager is to help people work through them as efficiently as possible. To do this, some of the tasks you have to achieve are to

- define the tasks that need to be done

- create management systems to help accomplish the tasks

- develop strategies for gaining commitment from employees

- develop communication strategies

- invite employee participation in the development of new processes and policies

- assign employees, resources, experts, and consultants to manage the change

- study present conditions

- collect data on employee attitudes toward the change

- create models of the end state

- state the goals of the transition and clearly describe the end state.

Project Management

Project management consists of planning, organizing, and controlling work. The goal of project management is to deliver a project that is on time, within budget, meets the required performance or specification level, and uses resources wisely. A project manager plans for a project's needs and then organizes and controls project resources as it progresses. Your tasks in managing projects are defined in the following sections.

■ *Defining the Project and Goals*

Regardless of the specific project goals and end deliverables, you, as project manager, are responsible for

- ensuring that the project work, and only the approved project work, is completed (scope)

- ensuring that the project schedule is planned, communicated, and monitored

- tracking an initial project budget and expenses incurred as the project progresses

- measuring and monitoring that the project deliverables meet the specified quality guidelines and standards

- scheduling and managing the appropriate use of resources.

■ *Project Planning*

The next task is establishing a plan for how the project will be accomplished. These are the steps in this process:

1. Select a strategy for achieving the objective.

2. Divide the project's tasks into subtasks and units (the work breakdown structure [WBS]).

3. Determine the standards for measuring the accomplishment of each subtask (specifications).

4. Develop a time schedule and sequence for performing tasks and subtasks (Gantt charts and program evaluation review technique [PERT] charts—also known as the critical path method [CPM]).

5. Estimate costs of each task and subtask and compile the entire project's cost budget (if not determined).

6. Design the staff organization needed to fulfill tasks and subtasks, including the number and kind of people required, their duties, and any necessary training.

7. Develop policies and procedures that will be in effect during the project's life cycle.

8. Acknowledge predetermined parameters imposed by the customer or organization, such as military standards or specifications.

Then carefully detail and document each element.

■ *Staffing a Project and Project Roles*

During the planning process, you compiled the tasks and subtasks that need to be performed. An important element of planning is finding and using the correct personnel to perform these tasks. Usually, in the interests of cost, time, and availability, you can find the personnel for a project within the organization. However, project managers often have the option of hiring expertise from outside the organization; hiring a consultant, for example, may be the best way to obtain the required skills without hiring full-time employees.

■ *Managing a Project*

You can use a variety of tools to prepare schedules and track work on a project. The following are three of the most important:

- The WBS not only identifies tasks, subtasks, and units of work to be performed, but also assists in estimating and tracking costs of each of these elements. A WBS represents a graphical hierarchy of the project, deliverables, tasks, and subtasks.

- A project's timeframe is derived from the plan and the WBS. The project manager lists the WBS components, arranges them in sequence, and determines how the elements mesh to form a milestone chart. Timeframe data is mapped into a chart called a Gantt chart, which graphically displays the time relationships of the project's steps and key checkpoints or deliverable dates, known as milestones. It's a valuable tool for project managers in planning, monitoring, and controlling projects.

- PERT and CPM charts are two widely used network-diagramming techniques. Network diagrams plot a sequence of activities (predecessor and successor tasks) to illustrate the interrelationships among activities and resources. PERT and CPM are also used to calculate the project duration.

Communication

Communication is an important competency in all areas of a manager's job, from presenting plans to executives, to interacting with subordinates, to communicating change initiatives, and more. Some facets of communication that a manager must master include presenting, listening, and giving feedback.

Presenting

In business, presentations are a fact of life. They can range from brief presentations to the executive team to a series of talks that constitute a training program. In any case, giving a presentation can be pretty frightening. *Communication Basics*'s authors Judy Jenings and Linda Malcak provide four steps to presentation success:

1. Focus on the participants. Find out who will be there and why, what they need to know and how they want to hear it, what makes them feel comfortable or uncomfortable.

2. Focus on the content. Now that you know who will be there, you know what kind of information they need and want to hear and how they prefer to hear it. Especially try to find out what the audience's pain points are and how what you have to say can relieve those pain points.

3. Focus on the structure of the presentation. Now that you know whom you are talking to and what you need to say to them, it's time to prepare your roadmap for how you are going to say it. Create an agenda that shows you where you stop and start, where you move on to a new topic, and where you provide breaks (if necessary). Then practice. And practice some more.

4. Finally, follow your plan. If you have focused on the right things by following the other three steps, then you can carry off your presentation with confidence.

Listening

The ability to listen well may be one of the most underappreciated and most powerful communication skills that anyone could have. Lyman K. Steil's sensing, interpreting, evaluating, and responding (SIER) model of listening is an effective method to ensure that you take full advantage of the ability to capture the full gist of that person's message before you respond. A brief description of the model follows.

■ ***Sensing***
To listen effectively, you must first receive the message accurately. That means being silent and allowing yourself to hear what the other person has to say. But hearing the words is only one component of sensing the other person's message. You've also got to pay attention to the person's body language, tone of voice, and pattern of breathing.

■ ***Interpreting***
Successful sensing lays the groundwork for the interpreting stage of the Steil SIER model. This is the stage in which you interpret the speaker's meaning. Considering the variety of meaning in words and the different ways that people use body language, this may be the most difficult stage of listening. To help you interpret correctly, rephrase what the speaker has said or ask for further clarification.

■ ***Evaluating***
Only after you have fully sensed and interpreted the message are you in the position to evaluate it. This involves understanding your own reaction to the message: Did you like it? Dislike it? Think it was poorly argued? Think it was complete or incomplete?

■ ***Responding***
The final stage of the model is responding. However, people often skip ahead to this point without taking the time and the focus to gather important information from the message along the way.

Giving Feedback

Feedback is a learned skill. Mastering its use can help you

- learn continually
- strengthen your communication skills
- develop more effective relationships
- improve your decision-making capabilities
- take advantage of opportunities for growth.

In your role as a manager, feedback is important in coaching, delegating, and managing performance. The sidebar *Giving Feedback* at right describes an effective feedback process.

Personal Effectiveness

Personal effectiveness is what enables you to stay organized, use your time effectively, and stay on top of your work.

■ *Time Management*

One way to get control of how you use your time is to keep a log of what you do for several days by writing down each task change that you make. Then review the log and determine if there are any obvious time wasters and work to eliminate them.

In "A Get-Real Guide to Time Management," Donna J. Abernathy cites research into time thieves that include telephone calls, drop-in visitors, lack of necessary resources, personal disorganization, indecisiveness, an inability to say no, procrastination, paperwork, and management by crisis. Once you have identified your biggest time wasters, determine ways to eliminate or minimize their effect. For example, if phone calls are your greatest time thief, set aside a portion of the day during which you send all calls into voicemail.

■ *Planning*

Closely related to time management skills are planning and prioritizing skills. To get the most of your time, practice focusing on the things that really make a difference at work. Abernathy describes the following categories to help you sort your work:

- A priorities: If you had nothing to do today, what should you work on that would improve your productivity in one to four weeks? What items on your to-do list are most closely related to organizational goals and strategies?

- B priorities: What things must be done today? Can you delegate any of them?

- C priorities: What things should be done today or tomorrow? Can you delegate any of them?

- D priorities: What things should you not do at all? (This may be the time to delegate, or you may want to let go of the item altogether.)

Giving Feedback

To be effective, feedback must be expressed in a manner that helps the receiver hear the message while keeping the relationship intact. To accomplish these goals, you must do the following:

■ *Show consideration*

One of the objectives of feedback is to help someone, not hurt someone. For that reason, you need to give feedback with care. To show consideration while giving feedback

- monitor your behavior
- practice active listening
- express concern and caring.

■ *Withhold judgment*

To reduce the receiver's resistance to feedback, make sure that you withhold judgment. Don't evaluate the behavior, don't assume its intent, but do describe specific behavior and its effects or consequences.

■ *Deliver at an appropriate time*

Most feedback literature states that you should give your message immediately after the behavior takes place or the next time there is a potential for recurrence. Generally speaking, this is the right approach to take. However, there are occasions when waiting is appropriate. One example is when either you or the receiver may lose emotional control. Another example is when the physical setting is inappropriate.

■ *Provide freedom to change or not*

It is important to acknowledge that the receiver is free to change or not. That decision belongs solely to him or her. However, make the effects of the behavior clear, because these effects may not be what the receiver intended. In addition, make clear what the consequences of continuing the behavior will be, whether positive or negative.

■ *Check for readiness*

Ideally, you should give feedback only when the receiver is mentally, emotionally, and physically ready to receive it. Feedback tends to work best when the receiver is open to it. However, circumstances aren't always ideal, and you may need to give feedback even when the receiver doesn't want to hear it. In those cases, double check your motivation: Do you want to give feedback, or are you just angry and want to sound off?

■ *Check for clarity*

Finally, check with the receiver to make sure that the message he or she received is the one that you intended to send.

Adapted from Holly DeForest, Pamela Largent, and Mary Steinberg's "Mastering the Art of Feedback," Infoline No. 250308.

■ *Organization Skills*

According to David Allen in *Getting Things Done,* "[h]aving a total and seamless system of organization in place gives you tremendous power because it allows your mind to let go of lower-level thinking and graduate to intuitive focusing, undistracted by matters that haven't been dealt with appropriately." One way to free up your mind for higher-level thinking is to empty your in-box regularly and use an efficient process.

Allen describes a simple process to empty your in-box regularly (and it applies to email also):

● Pick up or open the first item first. Don't look at any other items.

● Decide if you have to do anything with the item (whether now or later). If not, determine if you want to throw it out or file it for reference and do so immediately.

● If you do have to do something, determine exactly what that is, including any substeps. The action you decide on should be the next possible thing that you can do. For example, if you have received a tax form, and you realize that you need to file your taxes but you haven't received your W-2s, your next step may be to call your human resources department to get a copy.

● Then, determine how to do it. If it's an action that will take less than two minutes, do it immediately. If it will take longer than that, decide whether to delegate the task or do it yourself. If you need to do it, put a reminder into your schedule and file the paperwork. Never put anything back into your in-box.

■ *Problem Solving and Decision Making*

Solving problems and making decisions make up much of the day-to-day work of managers. Here is a six-step method for doing this that enables you to consider multiple options:

1. Define the problem. Simply stated, a problem is a discrepancy between what is and what should be. State the problem in the form of a question; for example, "How can we reduce the number of errors on the production line?"

2. Analyze the problem.

3. Establish a checklist of criteria use in evaluating potential solutions.

4. List all possible alternatives (it can be helpful to get input from employees who are also involved in the problem).

5. Select the alternative that aligns best with the checklist of criteria and determine how to implement the solution.

6. Implement the solution. Monitor and evaluate the solution to ensure that it solves the problem.

■ *Influencing*

Basically, influence is communicating with the purpose of gaining support for your ideas. To exert influence over others, there are two habits you must develop. First, seek to understand what the other person wants (his or her priorities) and how he or she operates.

Second, examine how your own priorities may blind you to options. Although it is difficult to be objective, doing so liberates you to be more effective with others by enabling you to base discussions on organizational priorities.

When you can listen to others and understand what they want and what you should avoid, you will be able to predict more accurately their priorities and influence their decision making.

Move Forward

This *Infoline* provided a self-assessment to help you identify areas where you could use some improvement as a manager and brief overviews of some management competencies. This is only a beginning. As a manager, you must learn to embrace continual self-development. Start by identifying a competency or a skill to work on, practice the steps provided in this *Infoline* related to that skill, and look to the references and resources for more information. This is just your first step toward becoming a better and more efficient manager.

References & Resources

Articles

Abernathy, Donna J. "A Get-Real Guide to Time Management." *Training & Development,* June 1999, pp. 22-25.

Buckingham, Marcus. "What Great Managers Do." *Harvard Business Review,* March 2005, pp. 70-79.

Gosling, Jonathan, and Henry Mintzberg. "The Five Minds of a Manager." *Harvard Business Review,* November 2003, pp. 54-63.

Haneberg, Lisa. "Reinventing Middle Management." *Leader to Leader,* Fall 2005, pp. 13-18.

Hogan, Robert T., and Jorge E. Fernandez. "Syndromes of Mismanagement." *Quality and Participation,* Fall 2002, pp. 28-31.

Kaye, Beverly L., and Sharon Jordan-Evans. "The ABCs of Management Gift-Giving." *Training & Development,* December 2000, pp. 51-52.

Liccione, William J. "Balanced Management: A Key Component of Managerial Effectiveness." *Performance Improvement,* February 2005, pp. 32-38.

Lippitt, Mary. "How to Influence Leaders." *Training & Development,* March 1999, pp. 18-22.

McCrimmon, Mitch. "How Not to Waste Money on Leadership Development." *OD/Leadership News,* March 2006. Available at http://www.astd.org/astd/publications/newsletters/od_leadership_news.

McLagan, Patricia. "Management by Intent." *Leader to Leader,* Fall 2004, pp. 12-15.

Mittler, James E. "It's Management Quality That Matters—Not Style." *Quality and Participation,* Fall 2002, pp. 19-21.

Raudsepp, Eugene. "How to Delegate Effectively." *Machine Design,* April 20, 1995, p. 11.

Tulgan, Bruce. "The Under-Management Epidemic." *HRMagazine,* October 2004, pp. 119-122.

Books

Allen, David. *Getting Things Done: The Art of Stress-Free Productivity.* New York: Penguin Group.

ASTD (American Society for Training & Development). *ASTD Learning System.* Alexandria, VA: ASTD Press, 2006.

Blanchard, Ken, and Steve Gottry. *The On-Time, On-Target Manager.* New York: HarperCollins, 2004.

Blanchard, Kenneth, Patricia Zigarmi, and Drea Zigarmi. *Leadership and the One-Minute Manager.* New York: William Morrow, 1985.

Flaherty, Jane S., and Peter B. Stark. *The Competent Leader: A Powerful and Practical Tool Kit for Managers and Supervisors.* Amherst, MA: HRD Press, 1999.

Haneberg, Lisa. *High Impact Middle Management.* Avon, MA: Adams Media, 2005.

———. *Coaching Basics.* Alexandria, VA: ASTD Press, 2006.

Handy, Charles. *21 Ideas for Managers.* San Francisco: Jossey-Bass, 2000.

Jenings, Judy, and Linda Malcak. *Communication Basics.* Alexandria, VA: ASTD Press, 2004.

Radde, Paul O. *Supervising: A Guide for All Levels.* Austin, TX: Learning Concepts, 1981.

Russell, Jeffrey, and Linda Russell. *Strategic Planning Training.* Alexandria, VA: ASTD Press, 2005.

Steil, Lyman K., and Richard K. Bommelje. *Listening Leaders™: The Ten Golden Rules to Listen, Lead & Succeed.* Edina, MN: Beaver's Pond Press, 2004.

Infolines

Battell, Chris. "Effective Listening." No. 250605.

Darraugh, Barbara. "Coaching and Feedback." No. 259006 (revised 1997).

DeForest, Holly, Pamela Largent, and Mary Steinberg. "Mastering the Art of Feedback." No. 250308.

Estep, Tora. "Meetings That Work!" No. 250505.

Gaines, Kathryn. "Leading Work Teams." No. 250602 (revised 1998).

Gilley, Jerry W. "Strategic Planning for Human Resource Development." No. 259206.

Grosse, Eric F. "Interview Skills for Managers." No. 250206.

Hickman, E. Stewart. "Hiring and Retaining Top-Performing Employees." No. 250011.

Lauby, Sharlyn J. "Motivating Employees." No. 250510.

Verardo, Denzil. "Managing the Strategic Planning Process." No. 259710.

Wircenski, Jerry L., and Richard L. Sullivan. "Make Every Presentation a Winner." No. 258606 (revised 1998).

Younger, Sandra Millers. "How to Delegate." No. 259011 (revised 1997).

Better Manager IDP

To prepare your IDP, determine where you require additional development using the Management Competencies Self-Assessment. Write the competencies down in the following table. Then rank them. Give the one that is costliest to you and/or your organization the number 1, the next costliest the number 2, and so forth.

Competency Area	Description of Costs (Personal and/or Organizational)	Rank Order
Business Management		
People Management		
Process Management		
Communication		
Personal Effectiveness		

Next, create a table with the following headings to prepare your IDP (you can use a word processing program, a spreadsheet program, or simply write by hand—whatever format is most comfortable for you). Leave plenty of space to write your goals. In the first column, write the name of the management competency. In the second column, identify activities to help you improve your skills in the competency area. Make sure that these follow the SMART goal format: they should be **s**pecific, **m**easurable, **a**ttainable, **r**ealistic, and **t**ime bound. Use the third column to keep track of progress on your goals. In the fourth column, list some ways to apply your new knowledge or some new habits to form that will improve your skills in this competency. The first rows have been filled in with an example to help you get started. Aim to make some progress every day, even if it is something minor like purchasing a book on a relevant topic.

Competency Area	Goals (Are they SMART?)	Progress	Ideas for Application
Process Management	Complete change management training offered through the organization's training department by 5/12.	Change management course completed 5/12	Prepare communication strategy to help people transition to the new paradigm.
	Read *Infoline* on meeting management by 6/18.	In progress	Prepare an agenda for every meeting.
	Complete project management training offered by training department by 8/15.	Submitted training request to training department	